# It won't work!

By Janine Amos and Annabel Spenceley
Consultant Rachael Underwood

CHERRYTREE BOOKS

A Cherrytree Book

Designed and produced
by A S Publishing

Copyright this edition © Evans Brothers Ltd 2003
by Cherrytree Press Ltd
327 High St
Slough
Berkshire
SL1 1TX

First published in 1999

First published in paperback 2003

*British Library Cataloguing in Publication Data*

Amos, Janine
  It won't work!. – (Good friends)
  1.Friendship – Pictorial works – Juvenile literature
  I. Title II.Annabel Spenceley
  302.3'4

  ISBN 1 84234 155 3

Printed and bound in Malaysia

# The sandcastle

Jacob is at the seaside with his grandad.
He is building a sandcastle.

Jacob fills his bucket with sand.
He pats it down hard.

5

He turns the bucket over . . .
and the sand falls out.

"Agh!" screams Jacob.
"It won't work!"

Jacob stamps his feet.
He bursts into tears.

Grandad puts down his paper.
"You sound very angry, Jacob," he says.

Jacob screams even louder.

"I can't do it!" he sobs.
**How does Jacob feel?**

"You're having a hard time building with
this sand," says Grandad.

"Yes," agrees Jacob, "it keeps falling out."

"What could you do?" asks Grandad.
Jacob thinks.

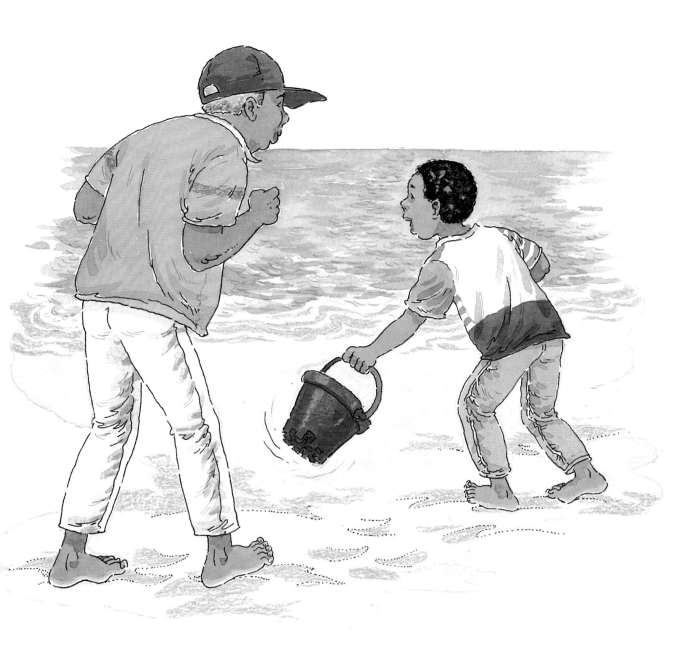

He looks at the sand. He looks at the sea. "I'll make the sand wetter!" says Jacob.

Jacob mixes sea water into the dry sand.

"Will it work now?" he wonders.

"I've done it!" smiles Jacob.
**How does Jacob feel now?**

# The marble game

Alice is playing with her marble game.
She fixes the pieces together.

She finishes the last tower.
Now she's ready to send down a marble.

Plop! – the marble drops to the bottom.

"It won't work!" thinks Alice.
**How does Alice feel?**

"What can I do?" she wonders.
She looks hard at the towers.

25

She checks each part.

"Yes!" says Alice, "here's the problem!"

She turns the yellow part around.

Alice tests the game again.

This time the marble rolls backwards and forwards all along the run!

31

Sometimes things don't work in the way we want them to. We feel frustrated or angry. It's OK to feel upset when things go wrong.

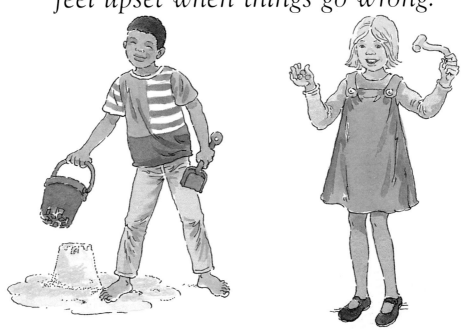

If something's not working, be a good friend to yourself; take a deep breath and tell yourself that you can do it. Looking at the problem again may help you to solve it. If you feel very upset, talk about it with someone else.